TO SAIL NO MORE

NO MORE

PART THREE

F 41

MIKE CRITCHLEY & STEVE BUSH

Introduction

As promised in Part 2 of this series we can now continue our clockwise tour around the UK naval ports & ship breaking yards. In this edition, we resume our journey at Inverkeithing.... visit some east coast yards and conclude at Portsmouth, where many vessels were, and are to this day, laid up whilst a decision is taken regarding their fate.

After months of sifting through readers photographs and researching captions one thing has become crystal clear; there is a treasure trove of material showing these vessels embarking on their final, sometimes epic, journeys to the ship breakers. We have been surprised at the interest this series has evoked - doubtless from old officers and men wanting to see how "their" old ship ended its days.

We have tried to capture a cross section of ships and ports throughout this book, from the great battleships being broken up at Inverkeithing, to the smallest minesweeper spending its final days as a perch for the local seagulls on the mud flats of the River Medway......from the scrapping of the wartime light fleet carriers to the post war Reserve Fleets in the United Kingdom and Malta. Many of the ships within these covers had long and distinguished wartime careers, whilst others, ordered during the war, found themselves surplus to requirements relatively quickly and spent many years languishing in reserve before a call to the ship breakers finally came.

Today (2000), with the expense of preserving vessels for further service, ships are not placed in reserve - just laid up pending sale or disposal. There is very little ship breaking left in this country. Increasing Health and Safety legislation and the labour costs of dismantling, (and with the frequently low value of scrap arisings) makes it a very marginal business venture. Despite UK workers from this "cinderella industry" being laid off, more and more we see redundant hulls being towed on long journeys to Spanish, Turkish and Far Eastern Yards where labour is cheap and "safe practice" appears not to be an issue.

The practice of using old hulls as targets during major naval exercises may also be a thing of the past as the "green lobby" becomes both vocal and powerful - and the advent of high tech computer modelling makes it unnecessary to destroy these ships on the high seas. So what does the future hold for these tired hulls? There is a growing worldwide trend towards sinking some of these vessels close offshore for use as recreational dive wrecks. The ships are stripped and dive routes opened up inside. They are totally surveyed to ensure that they are environmentally friendly and then scuttled. Already warships are in such use in the USA, Canada and Australia. There are moves afoot to do something similar in the UK. At least in this way a few ships will survive beyond the breakers torch and even whilst lying on the sea bed can bring economic benefit to the communities close to a dive site!

This is a book full of sad images. Ships that were once thriving communities, their every need attended to by scores of highly trained personnel; once lovingly painted and maintained highly efficient weapons of war. Within these covers we see them strangely quiet, deserted by those who once lavished attention on them and called them home. These pictures are able to evoke memories of days long since passed. Hopefully some of these images will stir memories of warmer sunny deployments to the tropics, while others may bring back experiences of long hard days of action during conflict - from Cod Wars to Confrontation in the Far East. Recollections doubtless remain of proudly manning the decks whilst entering a foreign port under the gaze of hundreds of people ashore, the White Ensign flying from the stern. Doubtless these are memories many readers would prefer to keep rather than those portrayed here.

This volume was made possible in the main by WARSHIP WORLD readers who have submitted hundreds of photographs over the past few years so that we could proceed. They have waited patiently whilst more photographs were collected to complete this book. We thank them all.

Whatever thoughts are stirred as you look through this volume, we hope you enjoy this collection of unique photographs - and if you have yet more good quality pictures on this theme, do let us see them. We could be tempted to publish more.................

Mike Critchley & Steve Bush   *Liskeard September 2000*

RODNEY in March 1948 having just arrived at Ward's Inverkeithing yards deep water wharf. Still sporting her wartime camouflage she was berthed alongside the remains of the liner GENERAL OSORIO. Within 21 months she would be totally broken up. (Thomas Ward)

Two leviathans of a past era silently await the scrapmans attentions at Wards on 6 March 1950. ROYAL SOVEREIGN (inboard) and REVENGE were amongst the last of the pre World War Two battleships to be scrapped. (Thomas Ward)

The remnants of REVENGE.....the bridge, spotting top and high angle director still standing despite part of the superstructure already having been demolished. To the left of this 1949 picture can be seen one of NELSONs three 16" barbettes. (T.W. Ferrers-Walker)

Looking forward over the 15" turrets. The barrels of A turret have already succumbed to the acetylene burners. (T.W. Ferrers-Walker)

After five years laid up in the Solent the carrier FORMIDABLE arrived at Inverkeithing on 12 May 1953 having been towed from Spithead on 7 May by the tugs ENGLISHMAN, TRADESMAN and SEAMAN. (Thomas Ward)

Just over a fortnight after arrival, this view of FORMIDABLE (taken on 30 May 1953) already shows evidence of the scrapmans presence with sections removed from the port bow. (Morris Allan)

A good aerial shot of Wards at Inverkeithing on 15 May 1954. By then the Battleships had been reduced to scrap and the yard was breaking up merchantmen. The two funnelled liner occupying the deep water berth is probably the P&O vessel MOOLTAN. Having seen service as an Armed Merchant cruiser and troopship during the war, she was returned to her owners in 1949 and eventually went for scrap in 1954. (Morris Allan)

The fleet carrier IMPLACABLE arrived at Inverkeithing on 5 November 1955, looking in remarkably good condition compared to FORMIDABLE which had been in reserve for 5 years. Inboard is the Troopship EMPIRE TROOPER. (Morris Allan)

9

Having been the only KGV class vessel to be laid up at Devonport, HOWE arrived at Inverkeithing on 2 June 1958. In this view she was being assisted by the tugs IMPETUS, FLAMER and ENERGY astern. (Morris Allan)

Unfortunately on arrival off Inverkeithing she grounded south of the entrance channel. Her deep sea tugs, WELSHMAN and ENGLISHMAN got her off the next day but due to fog she was unable to berth until the 4th June. (Morris Allan)

MONTCLARE pictured on 7 March 1958 having arrived in January for breaking up. A former Canadian Pacific passenger liner launched in 1921 she served as an Armed Merchant Cruiser after being requisitioned on 28 August 1939. Purchased in 1942 she saw further service first as a Destroyer Depot Ship and post war as a Submarine Depot Ship. (T.W. Ferrers-Walker)

An undated picture of MONTCLARE with demolition well advanced, most of the upperworks having been removed. The lack of HOWE outboard would date this picture before 4 June 1958. (Thomas Ward)

In this aerial view taken on 14 June 1958 HOWE is seen outboard of the depot ship MONTCLARE which had arrived in January and whose upperworks have already been removed. (Morris Allan)

The following three photographs are all various views of HOWE taken on 4 August 1958. Looking aft at the main armament and bridge she still looks pretty much intact. Berthed outboard is the frigate LARGO BAY which arrived for scrapping on 11 July. (D.G. Thomas)

15

A view of the after 14" quadruple turret, unique to this class, with the AA armament still "kooncoted" (D.G. Thomas)

This time looking aft, towards the entrance to Wards yard from the sea, from on top of the aft turret at the vast expanse of the teak timbered quarterdeck. The wood was also recycled so someone somewhere may have a table made out of this! (D.G. Thomas)

In this view dated 1 November 1958 HOWEs after funnel had been removed. Her mainmast had gone by the 5th. (Morris Allan)

Laid up on the Forth since 1956 GLORY made the short journey to Wards on 23 August 1961, berthing at the deep water wharf outboard of two unidentified merchantmen. (Morris Allan)

A mixed group await demolition at Wards on 22 October 1962. From left to right are the Emergency War programme destroyers CONCORD and CHEVIOT both having arrived that day from Rosyth and the cruiser SWIFTSURE which arrived on 17 October 1962, her refit at Chatham having been abandoned. (D.G. Thomas)

Completed in April 1943 the Algerine class minesweeper COCKATRICE spent a varied 20 years in both Reserve and Operational Fleets. Refitted in 1958 as an A/S Escort and fitted with Squid whilst in reserve at Chatham. No longer required she ended her days at Wards in August 1963. (Jack Williams)

Maybe not as glamorous as the big battleships....but in the eyes of the scrapmen just another lump of metal to turn into steel ingots. Here COCKATRICE surrenders yet more steel. (Jack Williams)

Last of the big guns!.....After 20 years at Devonport as a Turret drill ship and later as a fender vessel and accommodation ship, the ROBERTS was towed to Inverkeithing for demolition in July 1965. She is pictured here on 4 September that year. Her twin 15" guns were the last in the Royal Navy - her sister ABERCROMBIE having been broken up in 1954 and the battleship VANGUARD in 1960. (Morris Allan)

Although devoid of much of her superstructure the classic destroyer lines of ARMADA can still be discerned. Completed just too late to see action in the Pacific war, she alternated between reserve and active service until finally paying off in 1960. Arriving at Inverkeithing on 18 December 1965 this picture shows her in February the following year. In the background is the liner MAURETANIA. (Deryck Swetnam)

BROADSWORD at rest at the Inverkeithing beaching ground on 28 October 1968. Following her naval career she became a trials vessel for Naval Constructional Research Establishment (NCRE) experiments at Rosyth being used for target trials and underwater tests. The reference booms that were used to show flex in the hull during underwater explosions can still be seen in place. To the right of the picture the white letter H is on what was left of her upturned stern after her trials! (D.G. Thomas)

Surviving well beyond most of her sisters of the Whitby class EASTBOURNE finally arrived at the breakers on 7 March 1985. She saw service in the Home Fleet, the Mediterranean and the Far East before refitting in 1962 to become a Dartmouth training ship with extra boats in 1972 she became a seagoing training ship for engineers before finishing her career as a harbour training ship at Rosyth. (Mike Critchley)

D-Day Veteran demolished....In the summer of 1986 the RMAS Mooring, Salvage and Boom Defence vessel UPLIFTER arrived at Rosyth to be demolished. Completed in 1944 she saw service during the D-Day landings. In 1985 she was holed on an underwater target alongside at Fraserburgh and needed to be salvaged herself before being towed back to Rosyth! (Mike Critchley)

How long before the scrapmans torch cuts into this hull?.......Launched on Trafalgar Day 1960 DREADNOUGHT, the Royal Navy's first nuclear powered submarine went on to serve for 19 years. Laid up in Chatham in 1982, she was towed to Rosyth on 13 April 1983, where she remains to this day (2000), whilst politicians and environmentalists debate the best method of storage/disposal of these surplus nuclear powered vessels. (Maritime Photographic)

One of the last of the Battle class, BARROSA spent her final 7 years laid up in Portsmouth. In this picture taken on 27 September 1973 the massive AKE-2 aerial for the Type 965 radar can be seen. This item of equipment alone weighed 4 tons. She eventually left Portsmouth in December 1978 to be broken up at Blyth. (Martin Rogers)

A grand old lady bows out.....Completed in May 1938 it was to be another 40 years before MAIDSTONE finally made it to the breakers yard. Extensively rebuilt at Portsmouth between 1958 and 1962 to enable her to support nuclear submarines, she served six years at Faslane until the new shore base was completed, leaving in January 1968. Another career change saw her as an accommodation and prison ship in Belfast for eight years before finally being declared surplus to requirements in 1977. She was seen here on 23 September 1978 at Wards. (Martin Rogers)

COQUETTE and SPARROW left Portsmouth on 25 May 1958 in tow of TRADESMAN and MASTERMAN respectively. They arrived at Charlestown on the Forth on the high tide of 26 May. Work to demolish SPARROW commenced in August and COQUETTE in December of that year. (T. W. Ferrers-Walker)

After service with the Royal New Zealand Navy BLACKPOOL was returned to the Royal Navy in 1971 and placed in reserve. Following removal of the 4.5" turret she left Portsmouth under tow for Rosyth to be used as a target ship, hence the tower forward. She was seen here on 1 September 1978 at J. A. Whites Yard on the Forth ready to be broken up (Martin Rogers)

Submarines for sale.....OBERON and WALRUS seen alongside Doiges Slip in Grimsby. Purchased by Seaforth Ship Repairers in February 1987 as a speculative venture and renamed SEAFORTH A and SEAFORTH B. They were moved to Immingham for resale, Malaysia being considered a likely purchaser at the time. Despite worldwide marketing exercises there was no interest in the vessels and by 1991 demolition had begun. (G.R. Thompson)

WALRUS was gradually dismantled. Here the forward section of conning tower has gone leaving the attack periscope still in situ. Internally these boats were in remarkably good condition. (G.R. Thompson)

Stripped of stores and fuel OBERON rides high in the water, externally intact, awaiting her fate. The sonar dome seems a popular perch for the bird population! Meanwhile WALRUS had had much of her forward fibreglass streamlining removed. (G.R. Thompson)

Sitting forlornly on the mud flats of the River Medway were the tattered remains of FISKERTON. Seeing service with the 104th Minesweeping Squadron (MSS) in the Mediterranean and the 6th MSS in the Far East she was placed on the disposal list in March 1970. She was seen here in 1977 being dismantled by Henderson-Morez Ltd at Dartford Creek. (R. Goodrum)

The DIAMOND sat awaiting demolition at Bloors Wharf, Rainham on 14 November 1981, the last of the Darings in Royal Navy service. Here she looked almost complete, the foremast having been removed whilst serving as a Harbour Training Ship at Portsmouth. (R. Goodrum)

Completed in 1952 DIAMOND saw service in Suez at 1956. Much of her later life was spent as a Harbour Training Ship at Portsmouth for HMS SULTAN personnel, surviving through the seventies. (R. Goodrum)

Despite a career which included collisions with the cruiser SWIFTSURE off Iceland in September 1953 and SALISBURY in the Channel in June 1964 and a period of 10 years at Portsmouth, her hull looks in remarkably good condition. (R. Goodrum)

In this view the ships twin 4.5" turrets dominate. The Darings, as completed, were very powerful ships, with three twin 4.5" turrets, 10 torpedo tubes and a reported top speed of 34 knots. The last true RN greyhounds! (R. Goodrum)

FITTLETON at Liguria Maritime, Sittingbourne Creek, in 1977. In collision with the frigate MERMAID on 20 September 1976, during a ship to ship transfer off the Dutch coast, she capsized, but remained afloat for several hours before sinking. 12 crew lost their lives. Raised and refloated she was towed back to Chatham on 11 October. Never repaired she arrived for scrapping a year later. The bent foremast bears testament to the tragic incident. (R. Goodrum)

A WW 2 veteran GRENVILLE was completed as a leader of the U class of Emergency War Design destroyers - seeing service at both the Anzio and Normandy landings. Receiving a full Type 15 ASW frigate conversion she ended her days as an ASWE trials ship. She was pictured here in March 1983 at Queenborough Breakers on the Medway. (R.Goodrum)

One month later and most of GRENVILLEs superstructure had been removed. Her original destroyer hull form was becoming more evident. (R. Goodrum)

LEOPARD looked deceptively complete in the mud at Dartford in 1977. Powered by diesels these vessels had long endurance, but slow speed, which proved to be their Achille's heel. Not able to keep up with the carrier groups they were designed to escort, plans to fit them with anti-aircraft missile systems were shelved and they were discarded in the late seventies although one continued in service in Bangladesh past the turn of the century. (R. Goodrum)

It was not always easy to reach a breakers yard. Here at Dartford in 1977, LEOPARD was seen with her stern cut off. This was done in order to get her up the creek because the ship was too long to make it "complete"! (R. Goodrum)

After leaving Portsmouth under tow on 18 April 1979 KEPPEL was seen here on the beaching ground at Liguria Maritime Ltd at Sittingbourne on 30th April. Designed as single shaft ASW vessels these small ships had no room to accept newer systems and so had the distinction of becoming the first class of post war frigates to be scrapped. (R. Goodrum)

A puzzler for our readers...A survivor of the once numerous Ford class of Seaward Defence Boats KINGSFORD was seen here in the early 1970s at Queenborough Shipbreakers on the River Medway. However ,was she actually scrapped? Our research shows that she was later sold for private use in Greece in 1981 by Marine Turbo Craft Ltd! (R. Goodrum)

Those who also serve.....RMAS tug CONFIDENT ended her days at Rochester after a 30 year career. Built in 1956 by A & J Inglis she was based at Devonport until 1957. She spent most of her active life in Gibraltar, returning to Portsmouth in May 1974. The last of her class, she was seen here on 12 August 1986. (R. Goodrum)

If its value for money that the taxpayer wants, then they got more than enough with this ship. Completed as a fast minelayer in June 1941 MANXMAN played a key role in the resupply of Malta during WW 2. She was eventually torpedoed in November 1942, repairs completing in 1945. Despite this she remained in service, in several roles, including an Engineering Officers' Training ship, until arriving at Newport to be broken up in 1972. She was seen here with the tug RESOLVE leaving Chatham on 23 September 1971. (Mike Lennon)

For almost ten years a feature of Chatham Dockyard TRIUMPH was pictured here on 9 December 1981 leaving the Medway for a Spanish breakers. Completed as a light fleet carrier in 1946 she went on to serve as a training carrier, a cadet training ship and a heavy maintenance ship. Preserved in good order in Chatham since 1972 awaiting the call to active service, she left for the breakers a mere four months before the Falklands War, where a vessel of this type was sorely missed. (R. Goodrum)

Right up the beach.....The frigate BRIGHTON was towed to the Medway for demolition arriving on 16 September 1985. First commissioned in 28 September 1961, she went on to become a founding member of a new NATO Squadron (later to become STANAVFORLANT) formed at Portland in 1968. Paid off into the Standby Squadron in 1981 she was cannibalised during the next four years to provide spares for her sisterships, retained in service following the Falklands War. The RMAS tug NIMBLE towed the veteran Type 12 from Rosyth to Damhead Creek. (M.J. Gaston)

Still recognisable in this 1995 view, the World War One sloop CHRYSANTHEMUM was reduced to scrap at Rochester. Built by Armstrong on the Tyne in 1917 she operated as a Q ship throughout 1918. The inter war years were spent as a target towing vessel for gunnery exercises in the Mediterranean, before becoming the London RNR HQ on the Thames in 1939, finally relinquishing the role in 1987 after 48 years! (R. Goodrum)

Marking the end of an era for the Royal Navy, the cruiser TIGER was eased out of Portsmouth on a misty 23 September 1986 bound for Spanish breakers. Completed as a conventional 6-inch gun cruiser in 1959, she entered refit in 1968 for reconstruction. When she emerged in 1972 her sleek cruiser lines had gone forever, the after end of the ship having been converted into a flight deck and hangar for four Sea King helicopters. (RN Photo)

In the mid-1960s the trots in Fareham Creek were home to many ships awaiting their final journey. In this picture taken on 27 August 1965 the submarines SEA SCOUT (left) and TALLY-HO can be seen berthed among the destroyers and frigates. Both were subsequently broken up at Briton Ferry in 1965 and 1967 respectively. (Mike Lennon)

Another shot taken on the same day shows LOCH LOMOND. One of a class of 28, these vessels represented the final product of wartime experience in anti-submarine frigate design and operation. Using prefabrication methods, a Loch class vessel was completed in an average of 10 or 11 months. After final service in the Far East LOCH LOMOND was eventually scrapped by Shipbreaking Industries at Faslane in 1968. (Mike Lennon)

The former RUSHEN CASTLE, seen here in Fareham Creek, survived into the 1980s. A successor to the Flower class she was completed in July 1943. Reduced to reserve post-war she was transferred to the Air Ministry on 26 September 1960. Following conversion at Blyth SB & DD Co Ltd she emerged on 21 December 1961 as the Weather Ship WEATHER SURVEYOR, a role in which she served until 1976. Converted in Manchester for use as a salvage ship at Portsmouth, she was withdrawn from service in 1982 and broken up the following year by Arie Rijsdijk Boss En Zonen at Hendrik-Ibo-Ambacht. (Jeremy Shaw)

One of 44 British built LST(3) class of landing ship, ANZIO was converted in 1955 to an LST(A) to enable her to carry heavy tanks. Approved for disposal in 1966, she was de-equipped and was seen here in Fareham Creek on 27 June 1969. She was sold to Spanish breakers in February 1970. (Mike Lennon)

A gaggle of Type 14s - in the foreground EXMOUTH, unique amongst the class being converted in 1966 to serve as a trials platform for marine gas turbines - a "world first" for a major warship. Re-emerging in 1968 with a radically altered profile, caused mainly by the gas turbines voracious appetite for air. She had a machinery fit of one Olympus and two Proteus gas turbines in place of the original steam plant. She paid off into reserve in December 1976. In this undated picture she awaited her final tow to Briton Ferry. She arrived in February 1979. (K. Harrow)

By the late 1980s the Ton class were paying off in ever increasing numbers. Here GAVINTON, CUXTON and UPTON sit in Fareham Creek on 1 July 1991. By the winter of that year they had all been broken up in Belgium. Ahead of them can be seen the Mooring vessel MANDARIN which was sold for further commercial service. (Walter Sartori)

59

This 1978 picture shows PALLISER, KEPPEL (see page 46) and the armaments carrier KINTERBURY at the buoys. PALLISER left Portsmouth under tow on 9 February 1983, but the tug failed, so she was laid up at Devonport for a further month before resuming her journey, arriving at Neath on 27 March 1983 to be broken up. (Jeremy Shaw)

Many of the vessels laid up in Fareham Creek were scrapped just a mile away at Pounds Shipbreakers in Portsmouth. ARTEMIS (on the left) and TIPTOE, sold to Pounds in 1972 and 1971 respectively, were seen here laid up awaiting breaking. ARTEMIS had sunk alongside at Gosport on 1 July 1971, being raised five days later. It wasn't until post 1982 however that she was finally broken up. (Roger Allen)

In this undated wintery picture of TIPTOE her paintwork shows the effect of 7 years at the buoys. Having been bought in 1971, she remained laid up until 1979 when demolition finally commenced. This boat had the distinction of conducting the last submarine torpedo attack of WW 2, on 2 February 1945 in the Java Sea. (Roger Allen)

RUSSELL lies half demolished on 13 June 1986. This hulk was moved under the road to the remains of Pounds yard to the west with very little overhead clearance, explaining the removal of all the superstructure! (Deryck Swetnam/Roger Allen)

Barely recognisable here in 1999 are the remains of the former Ton class coastal minesweeper SHERATON at Pounds Yard. To the left her stern has been removed and upended while the rest of the hull can be seen to the right, with the propellor shafts prominent. A chain saw was a vital piece of equipment in scrapping these vessels. (Pete Barrie)

Paid off on 31 July 1991 OTTER was sold to Pounds in 1992. In this picture taken on 15 October 1995 all of the fibreglass streamlining has been removed, leaving just the pressure hull and skeleton of the fin intact. (Richard Lindfield)

A prototype motor gun/torpedo boat, BOLD PATHFINDER was completed by Vospers in July 1953 and attached to the trials unit at HMS Hornet (Gosport). Approved for disposal in 1962 she was sold to Pounds on 21 May 1962. After a relatively short naval career she was seen here, pretty much complete on 10 December 1984....over twenty years after arriving! However, by 1986 she had been totally demolished. (Walter Sartori)

With scrap prices falling and increasing health and safety regulations in the UK, India and other Far East countries soon dominated the market for surplus warships. HERMIONE (left) and JUPITER were seen here in November 1998 at the start of their epic 10,000 mile tow from Portsmouth to India, towed by the ex RMAS tug ROLLICKER. The trio reached India in May 1999 seven months after starting their journey! Their scrapping could not have been a commercial success. (Barry Smith)

Not all surplus ships end up in a scrapyard. UNDAUNTED was sunk in the Atlantic, 300 miles SW of Gibraltar, after use as a target in November 1978. The damage here was the result of an Exocet missile fired from the guided missile destroyer NORFOLK. (RN Photo)

UNDAUNTED was returned to harbour in Gibraltar where the damage was cut away before resuming her final role and receiving a direct hit amidships. In an effort to obtain maximum use from the hulk, the nuclear powered submarine SWIFTSURE delivered the coup de grace with a torpedo to finally sink her. Of note was the helicopter platform on the stern, fitted for trials of the Saunders-Roe P531 helicopters, forerunner of the Wasp. (RN Photo)

New weapons systems are normally tested against old hulls to assess their effectiveness. Here DEVONSHIRE became the target for trials of the Sea Eagle air-to-surface missile in 1984, the damage is evident amidships. The damage to the stern was caused by a Tigerfish torpedo fired from the nuclear powered submarine SPLENDID. (RN Photo)

Only the forward section of ASHANTI remained as she rolled over to slip beneath the waves on 14 September 1988. Used as a target in the South West approaches she was struck first by Sub-Harpoon missiles and then Spearfish torpedoes from SCEPTRE and SWIFTSURE. (RN Photo)

One of the last warships to be built at Portsmouth, SIRIUS was finally expended as a target on 30 September 1998 following two days of trying by SPARTAN and MONMOUTH. The original sinkex date was much delayed due to pressure from environmentalists in the wake of the Brent Spar incident, in which the oil rig was to be sunk at sea at about the same time. In the light of advances in computer simulations and pressure from the green lobby the requirement for live "Sinkex" targets could be a thing of the past. (RN Photo)

Paid off into reserve at Portsmouth in September 1945 the Hunt class destroyer CLEVELAND was wrecked on 28 June 1957 near Swansea en route to be broken up at Llanelli. The wreck was eventually stripped down and blown up in situ on 14 December 1959. (D.G. Thomas)

Every First Lieutenants nightmare.....On 30 September 1952 whilst sheltering in St Ives Bay, Cornwall, WAVE's anchor chain snapped during a gale. She was blown on to the sandy beach, then on to rocks and finally the sea front quay. Of the 94 crew, 62 were taken off by breaches buoy. The remaining 32, including the officers remained onboard. The weather conditions hadn't abated that much when this photograph was taken. She was subsequently towed to Devonport for repairs and further service, finally ending her days on 4 April 1962 when she arrived on the Tyne to be scrapped. (Western Morning News)

Completed in November 1943 BERKELEY CASTLE was placed in reserve at Harwich from 1947-48. In February 1953 she was badly damaged when she capsized whilst in drydock at Sheerness during the East Coast floods. Later refloated she was eventually put up for disposal in 1955 and arrived at Grays (Essex) on 29 February 1956 to be broken up by T W Ward Ltd. (Authors Collection)

ACHILLES pictured after colliding in the English Channel in fog with the Greek supertanker OLYMPIC ALLIANCE on 12 November 1975 injuring four men. She limped to Portsmouth for assessment before heading to Devonport for permanent repairs, which were completed by March 1976. She paid off in January 1990 and was sold to Chile in September where she serves on (2000) as MINISTRO ZENTENO. (S Goodman Collection)

WARSPITE was sold for breaking on the Clyde in 1946. Leaving Portsmouth in April 1947 was the prelude to a dramatic final chapter in her long life. The tow parted on 20 April and the hulk was eventually driven ashore in Prussia Cove (Cornwall) on the 23rd. There she remained, gradually to be broken up in situ. It wasn't until 1956 that the final remains (50 tons of boilers which had sunk six feet into the sand) were blasted into fragments so small that they would be absorbed by the sand. (Aerofilms)

Completed as a 'U' class destroyer on 1 March 1944 by J. Thornycroft at Southampton URSA spent a year serving in Home and Pacific waters before paying off into reserve at Portsmouth and Chatham (1946-52). Converted to a Type 15 frigate (1953-55) she saw further service with the 6th Frigate Squadron (FS) in the Mediterranean (1955) and the 5th FS (1961). Her damaged bows were the result of a collision with BATTLEAXE during a night anti-submarine exercise on the Clyde. She was repaired and saw further service with the 8th FS (1963) before paying off at Devonport in October 1966, finally being towed to Newport to be broken up in September 1967. (Authors Collection)

A Weapon class destroyer built by Yarrow at Scotstoun completing on 23 October 1947 BATTLEAXE was converted to a Radar Picket (1958-59) and joined the 2nd Destroyer Squadron (DS). Joining the 5th DS in January 1961. Her seagoing career was abruptly ended following the collision with URSA. She was subsequently declared beyond economic repair. Approved for scrapping in 1963 and moored alongside the Naval Constructional Research Establishment (Rosyth). On 20 October 1964 she arrived at Blyth to be broken up. (Authors Collection)

HUBBERSTON was built at Fleetlands in Gosport completing on 14 October 1955. After seven years in reserve at Hythe she was converted to a minehunter at Chatham. She served from 1965 - 71 in the Far East and took part in the second Suez Canal clearance operation in 1975. Paid off at Portsmouth on 21 February 1991 she was towed to Bruges (Belgium) on 13 May 1992 for breaking up. Notice the chains passed through the hull to pull her up onto the beach and the mechanical claw that rapidly rips through the wooden hull. (Urbain Ureel)

CUXTON was one of the first of her class to be built, being completed in 1954. She spent her first 21 years in reserve, including 7 years at Gibraltar. She eventually commissioned into the 1st MCMS in 1975 and saw service with the Fishery Protection Squadron in 1977. Paying off on 23 March 1991 she too was towed to Bruges for breaking up on 16 April 1992. These two pictures were taken a mere five days apart! (Urbain Ureel)

CHILDERS was completed as a flotilla leader on 19 December 1945 as one of the Emergency War Design class of destroyers. Equipped for tropical service she served in the 14th DS in the Mediterranean returning to the UK in 1950. Laid up at Gibraltar in 1958 she eventually left on 14 September 1963 (in tow of the Dutch tug Noordzee), arriving La Spezia (Italy) on the 22nd for breaking up. (Mike Lennon)

Transferred to the Royal Canadian Navy on completion in 1944 HMCS SIOUX (ex VIXEN) underwent a limited Canadian style Type 16 AS frigate conversion. Decommissioning in 1965 she was finally towed by the Portuguese tug PRAIA GRANDE from Canada to La Spezia for breaking up. Seen here off Gibraltar on 13 August 1965 when the tug called for bunkers before continuing her long journey to Italy. (Mike Lennon)

Commissioned into the 108th MSS in 1956, MADDISTON spent 1958-61 in operational reserve at Aden. Seen here at Gibraltar after a refit in 1963 she was then placed in reserve. She arrived back in Hythe (Southampton) in June 1969 before her final tow to Kitson Vickers Ltd (Sunderland) on 4 February 1975 to be broken up. (Mike Lennon)

The boom defence vessel LAYMOOR laid-up in Gibraltar in 1982. RN manned and operated she was one of the first boom defence vessels designed and built after WW 2. She entered Gibraltar harbour to pay off on 23 November 1979, one of the last "RN" ships propelled by steam reciprocating engines. Originally to be named BARFLAKE, after one of the two BDVs lost in WW 2, she was finally expended in 1984 as a target. (Steve Bush)

After spending the last year of WW 2 on minesweeping operations in the Dardenelles and Eastern Mediterranean, ACUTE returned to UK and was laid up in reserve at Harwich in November 1946. May 1956 saw her recommissioned into the Dartmouth Squadron as a training ship before finally paying off in July 1961. Seen here (in 1964) being towed past Gibraltar en route to Malta to be expended as a torpedo target. She was finally scrapped at La Spezia in November 1964. (Mike Lennon)

Lazaretto Creek (Malta) in 1959 showing both operational and reserve ships. Identifiable units include the depot ship AUSONIA with the destroyer DAINTY to port and the LST LOFOTEN to starboard. Ahead of them is the destroyer CROSSBOW. The LST ANZIO is on the opposite side of the creek. You will need a very good memory or a magnifying glass to further identify the boom defence vessels and small craft! (Courtesy David Pickett)

The same group of ships, this time viewed from the opposite side of the creek reveals a Ton class coastal minesweeper and a seaward defence boat berthed alongside the LST LOFOTEN. (Courtesy Colin Rouse)

An undated photograph of Gzira Creek, Malta. The presence of the depot ship RANPURA with a Colony class cruiser alongside her port side and the Weapon class destroyer SCORPION lying astern probably dates the picture from 1955-56.

Gzira Creek again, from the other end. Prominent in this view are several Algerine class minesweepers, including SYLVIA, and several MLs. RANPURAs funnel is just visible in the centre background.

The last of the M Class - Ex MARNE, MATCHLESS, METEOR and MILNE await the scrapmans torch in Turkey. After several years spent in reserve at Penarth (S. Wales) the four ships were brought forward from reserve in 1957 and transferred to the Turkish Navy in 1959. D351 PIYALE PASHA (ex METEOR) and D352 ALP ARSLAM (ex- MILNE) (nearest the camera) can be identified. The destroyers arrived at MKE Scrapyard, Seymen, in July 1974 after being moved from Golcuk Naval base, some 2 miles to the west. Demolition was complete by 1976. (Selim San)

The sale of BERRY HEAD for scrap was somewhat complex. Built in Canada during WW 2 she was originally sold to Spanish breakers for approximately £500,000; but the Spanish company failed to come up with the money to complete the sale. The MoD then renegotiated the sale with Dido Steel Corporation of Athens who paid approx £300,000. The Greek buyer took the ship to Turkey to be broken up at Aliaga, where she was photographed on 21 March 1990. (Selim San)

Some light hearted humour as WASPERTON pays off. Completed as a minesweeper by Whites Shipyard, Southampton on 19 July 1957 she spent ten years (1958-68) with the Fishery Protection Squadron before entering Rosyth in 1971 for conversion to a patrol craft. She sailed for the Far East on 9 January 1972, arriving in Hong Kong on 28 April to join the 6th Patrol Boat Squadron. Replaced by the Peacock class in 1985 (RN Photo)

YARNTON and WASPERTON lie alongside the North Arm at HMS TAMAR, Hong Kong awaiting a buyer. Already stripped of their radar and 40mm Bofors guns, they being returned to the UK for further service. (Authors Collection)

The last of the Hong Kong "Tons" to be decommissioned in October 1985 was WOLVERTON. She ended her days as a floating night club in Hong Kong harbour. Opulently refurbished by a local millionaire she was known variously as the WOLVERTON CLUB, MANHATTAN CLUB and finally CLUB VENETIA. Reputedly used for illegal gambling she was gutted by fire in 1991 after a suspected arson attack. (Mike Lennon)

INDEX